VICTORIAN EDINBURGH

Frontispiece and Jacket
Tolbooth St. John's from Castle Hill

CASTLEHILL

VICTORIAN EDINBURGH

Written and Illustrated by

J. Brian Crossland

WAYFAIR PUBLISHERS LTD
LETCHWORTH

WAYFAIR PUBLISHERS LTD

8a Arena Parade
Letchworth
Herts.

●

First published 1966

This book has been set in Monophoto Plantin, and printed
in Great Britain by Morrison & Gibb Ltd., London and Edinburgh

For My Wife, Audrey

Acknowledgements

The Author wishes to thank the following persons and organizations for the help given him in compiling this book:

The invaluable resources of the Edinburgh Room at the Central Library
H.M. Ministry of Works
The Episcopal Church of Scotland, with particular thanks to the rectors of St. Peter's, Lutton Place and St. James', Leith
The Church of Scotland, with particular thanks to the minister of Tolbooth St. John's
The British Linen Bank
H.M. Register House
The managements of the King's Theatre and the Royal Lyceum Theatre
The Curator of the Royal Scottish Museum
The Headmaster of Donaldson's Hospital

For permission to reproduce the following drawings:

Mr. A. V. Gabra (St. Mary's Cathedral)
The National Commercial Bank
Mr. Grant (The Abbotsford)
Mr. Douglas Stewart (The Barclay Church and St. Leonards)
Mr. R. M. Munro (Donaldson's Hospital)
Mr. Henderson (Ramsay Gardens)
Lloyds and Scottish Finance Ltd. (Chester Street)
Mr. Bryan Johns (The McEwan Hall)
Mr. Michael Elder (St. Giles Street)
Messrs. Oliver & Boyd, for permission to reproduce 'Victoria Street', and to Mr. George Scott-Moncrieff, as this drawing is reproduced in his book *Edinburgh*

Finally, the Author wishes to express his sincere thanks to the many people who have written to give him rare and otherwise unobtainable information, and also to his secretaries for the considerable part they have played in interpreting his text.

Contents

The Drawings

Foreword

My Publishers, amongst others, have asked me how I came to write this book, and I think it is only fair to satisfy their curiosity.

A deep affection for the City of Edinburgh, coupled with an interest in architectural history, gave me a realization of the neglected qualities of many of the city's major buildings erected in the reign of Queen Victoria.

Some five years ago, The Scotsman Publications very kindly agreed to my suggestion for a series of articles and drawings on Victorian Edinburgh. This gave me the opportunity for a study whose interest grew with its increasing difficulty. It quickly became apparent that the popular conception of nineteenth-century architecture bore little relationship to the reality. Furthermore, the obscurity of nineteenth-century architectural history is remarkable.

The Victorians were adventurous and inventive and these qualities are easily seen in the architecture of the period. Regrettably, contemporary criticism was more enthusiastic than valid, and thus we have inherited absurdities in architectural description which inhibited twentieth-century appreciation of nineteenth-century style. I trust that I shall not be reproached for attempting a redefinition. I have also broken new ground in categorizing the Italianate Revival and I have also attempted a simplified definition of the Gothic.

There is much that is new here, especially in details of Victorian architects whose influence in the city has been obscured by the almost total lack of Victorian architectural history.

J. BRIAN CROSSLAND

Introduction

Edinburgh in 1837

THE late nineteenth century saw the most remarkable burgeoning of philosophy and the arts in Edinburgh. Imaginative conceptions in mechanical invention and social improvements also played their part in this golden age of the Scottish capital. A lasting memorial to this creative era is the New Town of Edinburgh, an example of flawless technique in civic art, unequalled in the world. Projected in the eighteenth century, development of the New Town carried on well into the nineteenth century and was the inspiration of the architects and planners who created the extension of the New Town to the west of the Queensferry Road.

The close of Queen Victoria's reign was the end of an epoch more easily defined in terms of history perhaps than its beginning. It cannot have been realized in 1837 that the young and inexperienced girl who came to the throne was to become Queen Empress whose influence was predominant in leading the British nation to greatness despite changing and troubled times. Nevertheless, the year 1837 has a significance in Edinburgh singularly suited to the purpose of this book. Our interest is more topographical than social and this is the year that we see the finality of the Greek Revival in Edinburgh architecture in the addition and completion of Playfair's R.S.A. Gallery. It is coincidental that in that year Samuel Swarbreck produced his lithographs of Edinburgh, each with its kilted Highlander: a valuable record of the period, familiar to many today.

This introduction is illustrated by a drawing of Bristo Street. We take a great jump in time and pass from the heritage of the golden age to Victoriana, as it is generally seen in fiction and romance. Here is a street full of accidents of character. Its outward appearance is nineteenth century, its shell eighteenth and nineteenth century. There is a harmony about this jumble of buildings which speaks of humanity. The lost history of its individual dwelling places is the true and living history of man's struggle with life. In one of these tenements lived the notorious Burke. It is strange that the story of his partnership with Hare should alone have survived among the resurrection men, the suppliers of human bodies for dissection. Disgrace lies not with the lowly resurrectionists, but the surgeon who disregarded whether the poor shell of humanity was ripped from its recent grave or hastened out of life to satisfy the waiting dissection table.

Within these buildings lived Thomas De Quincey. Even in the age of adventurous individuality De Quincey was regarded with the air of rather shocked incredulity reserved for the unusual and curious, though this extraordinary genius was highly regarded by his contemporaries for his qualities, not only intellectual but human. His drug addiction does not appear to have affected his intellectual powers, nor indeed his health to any great extent, for he lived

Bristo Street—a survival of atmosphere.

to the age of seventy-four, when the expectation of life was much less than it is today, notwithstanding his basically frail constitution.

It is difficult to recapture the atmosphere of 1837. Nothing of great consequence happened in Edinburgh that year and the proclamation of the Queen's succession is outstanding. Bristo Street stands in decayed but respectable circumstances contemplating the overpowering weight of its neighbours in destroyed George Square. It is not over-imaginative to suggest a comparison in dignity and humanity favouring the doomed street. The more reflective may recapture an echo of the rumbustious life of 1837 which with all its hardship held the individualism and adventure of the Victorian era.

Bristo Street as we see it today is a survival whose complement has been swept away by the development of the McEwan Hall. It is for a short space a fragment of the older Edinburgh known to our forefathers. In decay it has certain well-defined characteristics which we must regard while we may. Its unassuming qualities may serve as a foil to the more splendid architecture to be seen in the progress of this book.

1 : *The Cult of Medievalism*

The Gothic Revival

IT is a commonplace that the architectural ideals of any defined era are dis-regarded or even reviled in the period immediately following its decline. This process, accelerated in the twentieth century by the peculiar difficulties of the age, helped to achieve a remarkable misunderstanding of the values of Victorian architecture. The Victorians' lack of clarity in the definition of their architectural contributions heightened the obscurity. This is especially noticeable in appre-ciation of the Gothic Revival, though it is a tribute to the force and value of this movement that its serious study commenced in the early 1930's, though this interest was confined to a few farseeing minds and produced little effect until the middle of the century. Understanding of this movement is inhibited by its complexity.

Mid-eighteenth-century Inveraray Castle is an early example of the Romantic Gothic of the late eighteenth century and is no prelude to the Gothic Revival of the nineteenth century which has an entirely separate motivation. St. John's Church at the West End of Edinburgh, by William Burn, is a delicate interpre-tation of the last phase of medieval Gothic wherein the architect has not hesitated to use cast iron. This remarkable building is outside our period and not the Gothic Revival as we know it.

Augustus Welby Northmore Pugin was the outstanding leader whose sincerity diverted nineteenth-century taste from the prevailing classic in church architecture. The burning enthusiasm of Pugin, whose purity of Gothic conception owes as much to his deep religious conviction as to the brilliance of his architectural gift, ensured that the main trend of Gothic Revival was ecclesiastical. The off-shoots of Gothic in the domestic field were influenced by fashion and were not subjected to the conflict arising from the Oxford Movement and the Evangelical Revival. Pugin himself held that true Gothic derived directly from the liturgical requirements of Roman Catholic rubrics.

Pugin's great influence was continued beyond his lifetime by his distinguished disciple, Sir George Gilbert Scott. The huge volume of important work carried out by this architect has wrongly tempted many architectural historians to dismiss him as a career architect. Careful study of his work and writings dismisses this view absolutely. His generous appreciation of his collaborators and his vast knowledge of Gothic architecture, displayed in his written work, should be sufficient encouragement for an open-minded comparison of his compositions.

St. James' Church, Leith. It is not generally known that this is the work of Sir George Gilbert Scott. Rare in Scotland, it has a full peal of eight bells.

The Cathedral Church of St. Mary

The Misses Barbara and Mary Walker of Coates and Drumsheugh, willed their property to the Episcopal Church for the erection, endowment and funds of a Cathedral dedicated to the Blessed Virgin Mary. It was stipulated that no fewer than four architects should be invited to submit designs and in fact the adjudicating body selected six—three English and three Scottish. The competition was won by Sir George Gilbert Scott, a decision which I feel the lapse of time has reinforced. The foundation stone was laid on 21st May 1874 by the Duke of Buccleuch, and in 1879 the incompleted church was consecrated and the nave opened for services. The estimated cost of £110,000 had now been reached, but a further bequest enabled the Chapter House to be added in 1890. Later, the energy of Bishop Walpole in promoting public subscription throughout the Diocese made provision for the twin west towers to be erected in 1915 and 1917.

Sir George Gilbert Scott's ability to create huge architectural compositions, viewable and flawless from any angle, is admirably demonstrated in St. Mary's. His attention to scale and detail is equally seen in every part of the building, and particular attention may be given to the wrought iron screens in the chancel, contemporary in period, yet perfectly in harmony with the Gothic form. That this is no mere accident is amply demonstrated in much of the interior decoration of his Glasgow University building. An unusual design feature of St. Mary's is seen in the curving ribs sweeping up to a central roof point at the east end, tending to give the impression of a circular apse; whereas the lancet windows are set in a flat wall, thus conforming more to native practice than to the continental.

The Cathedral Church of St. Mary is a major architectural contribution to its period. Its qualities are timeless and comparable in its day and age with the best work of the devout age of ecclesiastical craftsmanship. Its full recognition awaits only the passage of time.

It is not possible to conclude the subject without reference to its exceptional siting. As a terminal feature to Melville Street it is incomparable. Viewed from almost any angle the building is satisfying and the effect of the three spires against the evening sky at the West End of Princes Street enriches the City of Edinburgh.

ST MARY'S CATHEDRAL

St. Mary's Cathedral—of supreme importance in its period.

Tolbooth St. John's

The commanding and beautiful spire which dominates the head of the Royal Mile and proves so effective a point of interest from numerous aspects and vistas in the City of Edinburgh, is proof of the value set on siting by Victorian architects. Augustus Pugin collaborated with Gillespie Graham in the creation of Tolbooth St. John's. It is one of the accidents of history that these two architects, living so far apart and differing so widely in their architectural aspirations, should have become such firm friends. The story of their meeting is one of true nineteenth-century romanticism.

Pugin's dedication to the cause of the land-rooted Gothic Revival did not minimize his love of the sea. Indeed he is said to have worn sailors' clothes on numerous occasions. It was while sailing his own small craft off the mouth of the Firth of Forth that he was shipwrecked, and his rescue and subsequent entertainment by Gillespie Graham founded a sincere attachment which resulted in their future collaboration. There is no doubt that Pugin's influence was considerable in creating this splendid spire and much of the Gothic detail. Gillespie Graham is better known for his sensitive appreciation of classical proportion.

The foundation stone of the church was laid by Queen Victoria on her first visit to Scotland in 1842. The church was completed in 1844 and was then known as the Victoria Hall in recognition of Her Majesty's gracious act; and it was the future meeting place of the General Assembly of the Church of Scotland. Prior to 1844 the General Assembly had met in St. Andrew's Church in George Street. This body continued to meet annually at the Tolbooth Church until the reunion of the United Free Church of Scotland in 1929; since then the present hall of the General Assembly has been used for the purpose. The full title of the church is 'The Highland Church of Tolbooth St. John's', although this style has been in use for less than a decade. Some thirty years ago the congregation of St. John's Church at the West Bow united with the congregation of the Parochial Church of the Tolbooth, and in 1956 the Highland Church vacated its building in Cambridge Street to join the United Congregation of Tolbooth St. John's. This is now the only church in Edinburgh where the sermon at the Sunday afternoon service is in Gaelic.

TOLBOOTH ST JOHN

The Highland Church of Tolbooth St. John's.

The Ecclesiologists

It is hardly surprising that Pugin's zeal in promoting Gothic architecture was unacceptable in some circles in view of his insistence that the Gothic led naturally to Rome. High Anglican opinion which found its expression in Tractarianism (the Oxford Movement founded by Newman in 1833) was disposed to accept Pugin's views, certainly initially. Moderate Anglican opinion proved to its own satisfaction that Gothic was the expression of Orthodoxy and that the Roman Church had debased the progress of Medieval Gothic. It was held that the purest form of Gothic was the 'Middle Pointed' or 'Decorated Style'. These opinions were enshrined in the formation of the Cambridge Camden Society (named, after 1846, 'The Ecclesiological Society'). This body concerned itself with all aspects of architecture and church appointment in its relation to Anglican Ritual. In 1841 it founded a Journal whose contents were devoted to advice or judgement on the general practice of Ecclesiastical architecture and regularly indulged in the most minute criticism of new churches which were being built in great numbers.

Pugin was of course right in regarding the Gothic form as basically suited to Catholic Ritual rather than the reformed Evangelical Church. The Georgian model, with its galleries and central pulpit, consistent with Presbyterian requirements, was carried by the Church of Scotland well into the nineteenth century and indeed accounts for the use of the Italianate style, so much more in accord with congregational needs.

The little church at Summerside Place, Leith, owes nothing to the Ecclesiologists and its Gothic Revival has a slightly Continental air, so often seen in Scotland, adding a timely reminder of the 'Auld Alliance'. It is with a sense of disappointment that we note that this nicely proportioned church has no apse at the east end, which the rest of the exterior seems to demand. We are even more put out on entering the church to find a disappointing arrangement of galleries, crammed unsuitably into a Gothic exterior. Only Frederick Thomas Pilkington (see Appendix 3) had the skill to combine medieval architecture with a liturgically suitable interior for the Church of Scotland.

The Episcopalian Church in Scotland proved a more fruitful field for ecclesiological views. The work of Sir George Gilbert Scott won the approval of the Ecclesiologists, though he himself was quite uninfluenced by their teaching. St. Peter's, Lutton Place, is the work of a London architect, Slater, whose design probably as nearly approaches the ecclesiological influence in creating a nineteenth-century Anglican church as reason and moderation would allow. The offset spire, absence of side chapels, familiar arrangement of nave, chancel and sanctuary are all typically nineteenth century. The general style of the interior has overtones of 'Middle Pointed'.

ST PETERS LUTTON PLACE

The interior of St. Peter's, Lutton Place.

The Disruption

The great upsurge of thought in the reign of King William IV had its counterpart in the increasing influence of the evangelical party in the Church Assembly. A leader in this movement was the redoubtable Doctor Thomas Chalmers, whose intellectual progress from his entry into the University of St. Andrews at the age of eleven was no less formidable than his deeply sincere concern for the poor and neglected. From 1828 to 1843 he occupied the Chair of Divinity in Edinburgh where his identification with Liberal thought, and success in the promotion of religious and charitable movements gave him a widespread authority. His central purpose was to make the Church of Scotland a supreme influence in spreading the Gospel and redeeming the lost.

Dr. Chalmers became leader of the evangelical party in the division of the Church of Scotland which ended in the Disruption of 1843. Some four hundred and fifty-one ministers out of a total of twelve hundred walked out of the General Assembly on a point of conscience, to found the Free Church of Scotland. Such courage inspires unqualified admiration. These men did not know when they would have a roof over their heads or food for their families in the weeks to come. Yet within four years the distinctive twin Gothic towers dominating the head of the Mound, together with more than seven hundred churches throughout Scotland, were justification of the faith of the seceding ministers. We should do well to reflect today that such adherence to principle may well assure material success. At the time of the Disruption, and until 1844, the Assembly met in St. Andrew's Church in George Street. In 1844 the Established Church Assembly was moved to the newly completed Tolbooth St. John's Church (see page 18).

The twin towers referred to are of course those of the New College founded by the Free Church for the theological training of its ministers. Incorporated in the building was the Free High Kirk (now the Divinity Library). The architect of the New College was William Henry Playfair, and it is a tribute to his extraordinary ability that Playfair produced so striking a composition in a style so far removed from his usual classicism. The skill with which he planned his site is most noticeable. It cannot be mere accident that the entrance courtyard of the building lies on the axis of the tower of Tolbooth St. John's: a bold conjunction which is highly effective when passing through the entrance gate.

The New College—a major contribution to the Edinburgh sky-line.

2: *The Italianate Revival*

Classical Refinement

IN the third century B.C., Periclean Athens established a sophisticated design system which has dominated western civilization to this day. It is said that the Romans physically conquered the Greeks, whereas the Greeks in their turn culturally reconquered the Romans. When the beginnings of Medieval Society emerged from the dark ages the earliest Gothic architecture is sometimes styled Romanesque; thus Gothic architecture has its roots in the Roman Empire. The development of Gothic followed its own ethos until, in fourteenth-century Italy, the Renaissance of learning rediscovered the culture of the ancient world and gave us an architecture adhering strictly to the principles of classic proportion, yet a strongly defined creative form inseparable from its period in time. The strict discipline of the Renaissance developed into the exuberance and drama of the Baroque which spread into most of Europe.

The nineteenth-century Italianate Revival was yet another phase of the classic whose enthusiasm had its foundation in Continental and especially Italian study by the architects of the day. Like the Gothic Revival, the Italianate was preceded by a movement allied but in no way connected. The Greek Revival of the early nineteenth century was rooted in the romantic age of literature and art which succeeded the Augustan Discipline. Its motivation was a rediscovery of Hellenic Greece. In Edinburgh the Royal High School is an outstanding example of this style, while equally important is the Burns Monument on Calton Hill which has its inspiration in the Choragic monument of Lysicrates.

The National Commercial Bank in George Street (previously the Head Office of the Commercial Bank of Scotland) is one example of the sure grasp of classical design which the architect David Rhind gave to the mid-nineteenth century. He was one of the truly great Victorians and contributed to Scotland something more than a Revivalist style, for his grasp of general principles is secure in his knowledge and appreciation of classical architecture. His buildings have that touch of timeless distinction which transcends mere revivalism, and his use of ornament has a conviction, which, allied to the practicability of his space planning, is the mark of architectural greatness.

Classical Refinement—The National Commercial Bank, George Street.

Venetian Palazzo

The Life Association of Scotland building is one of the most important architectural compositions of its style and period in the United Kingdom and is singled out for special mention by Russell Hitchcock in the standard work on nineteenth- and twentieth-century architecture. It is High Renaissance Italianate Revival and the façade is street architecture of the highest order. The building itself is set in the centre and hub of Princes Street, placed in happy conjunction with the New Club, maintaining precisely the right emphasis in the street frontage between Hanover Street and Frederick Street. Threatened with destruction, it is indeed to the credit of all concerned that at the time of writing the best advice prevails.

This building was erected in 1855–8, the architect being David Rhind. There is a persistent idea that Sir Charles Barry was in some way connected with the design. I do not hold this view myself; moreover the Life Association building is not listed in Barry's more important works. Furthermore he died in 1860 and it is most improbable that an elderly and eminent man would have been engaged in collaboration with a younger architect on such an important building without the fact being generally established. David Rhind died in 1883 but the date of his birth is uncertain.

We are not vexed by the problem of architectural definition of the Life Association of Scotland building. Its creator has drawn on his knowledge of the fourteenth century to produce a building wholly nineteenth century both in style and convenience: a tribute to the timeless skill of the designer and an ornament to the City of Edinburgh.

One of David Rhind's less known compositions is the monument known as the Craigentinny Marbles. The most extraordinary story relates to this mausoleum. William Millar, a leading figure in Edinburgh, married in his ninetieth year an English woman who was then fifty. The couple travelled extensively and their son William, later M.P. for Newcastle-under-Lyme, was born in Paris sometime towards the end of the eighteenth century. The son had the reputation of being a great eccentric, as well he might. By the provisions of his will he lies at the depth of forty feet on the north side of the Portobello Road, surmounted by David Rhind's classical memorial.

THE LIFE ASSOCIATION OF SCOTLAND.

The High Renaissance—The Life Association of Scotland Building.

North British and Mercantile Insurance Building

The North British & Mercantile Insurance building in Princes Street has recently been demolished. The seriousness of its loss must be measured against the architectural value of its replacement, for it was a building which was difficult to assess and viewed in isolation would not have been of primary importance. As street architecture, and within the varied façade of Princes Street, it was wholly acceptable and will almost certainly be missed for qualities of scale and suitability unlikely to be matched in 1966.

It was built to the design of the architect J. M. Dick Peddie, and is slightly out of our period, having been completed in 1905. It replaced the former Scottish office of the insurance company which was an acceptable but rather self-conscious Georgian building of 1842. This may have been a partial reconstruction in which the basic proportions of the original Princes Street were followed. Or it may have been a conscious attempt to adjust to these proportions with characteristically pronounced window margins and general failure of detailing understandable in an age totally out of sympathy with the eighteenth-century feeling. The same sort of thing may be seen in even greater degree in official buildings of the 1930's where the determination not to set a foot wrong effectually sterilized architectural design.

Assessment of the building is exceedingly difficult, as I have suggested. Perhaps like its predecessor it was too anxious to conform to achieve a true expression of its architectural period. It was confident without having the assured splendour of its contemporaries. It had nothing in common with the intricate style of its immediate predecessors in the Fin de Siècle mood. With its near correct proportioning, rustication in the lower storey, slightly disproportionate main doorway and modest swags and Tuscan embellishments, it may well have carried the first faint blush of official rectitude. I do not mean to damn by faint praise. The building's true qualities speak for themselves in the drawing. A building which is individual, and difficult to equate with its period, is at the mercy of the architectural historian when its age has not revealed its proper significance in the passage of time. The building has gone and future judgement can only rest on recorded illustration. This at best is academic, as the only way in which to evaluate architectural composition is in movement, seeing the physical three-dimensional effect in its relation to its surroundings in the normal manner of the passer-by.

The North British & Mercantile Insurance Building.

The New Register House

One of the less pleasing dogmas of the modern architect is a contempt for the revivalist styles of the nineteenth century. He would be well employed in following the example of his Victorian predecessors in travelling the continent making studies and drawings of the finest historic examples. From such study are gained the elements and basis of design, and from this store of knowledge the Victorian architect was able to create his buildings of distinction. The Italianate Revival is one of the main streams of nineteenth-century inspiration. The influence of the Italian Renaissance is seen in buildings of elegant classical proportions, but it may be equally detected in the later terraces of the New Town where classical detail is restrained or even completely absent.

Robert Mathieson's New Register House was begun in 1859. Robert Adam's splendid General Register House at the east end of Princes Street had reached its capacity by the middle of the century and the Act of 1855 requiring the compulsory registration of births accelerated the necessity for new accommodation. With characteristic Victorian foresight it was courageously and rightly decided to erect an entirely new building in the vicinity of the old one. The site selected was unpropitious, spanning the pre-New Town Gabriels Road, and it was not until the opening out of the frontage by the erection of the Café Royal that Mathieson's beautifully proportioned façade could be appreciated.

The wrought-iron gates are a splendid example, very characteristic of the period, and lead to a commanding stairway and the main entrance of the building. It is regrettable that the special planning needs of the interior should disappoint one with a blank wall immediately on passing through the doorway. Robert Adam's solution to a similar problem in the adjacent General Register House might well have proved a model in carrying the promise of the exterior into the interior planning of the building. However, the façade is incomparable and the relation of window openings to wall space is irreproachable. After all, this is what the vast majority of people see, and those who enter the building must accept the convention as this is indeed the crux of its real and true value.

THE NEW REGISTER HOUSE

The Italianate Revival—The New Register House.

31

The High Renaissance

Once again we are beset by the niceties of definition. The term Italianate may cover equally the rich three-dimensional classical architecture of the National Commercial Bank or the restrained proportions of the New Register House. Whilst admitting the generic term, one's interest is heightened by observing the differing approach that each architect has made to his subject.

It is necessary to employ a different critical view of buildings in which the influence of Renaissance study is dominant. It would be unwise to separate the monumental from the domestic; however, certain outstanding architects have wisely given us buildings of special prominence whose grandeur is suited to their importance and whose skill in execution may be equated with the High Renaissance. The McEwan Hall is such a building. It was completed in 1897 to the design of Dr. Rowand Anderson. His knowledge in his chosen field matches that of Sir George Gilbert Scott in the Gothic, and the grandeur of his compositions justified the leading position he held towards the end of the Victorian period. His site planning for the McEwan Hall is as remarkable as his detailing. It is a great pity that the Campanile which was proposed for the north side of the group, was never built.

We have examined David Rhind's strict and skilful interpretation of the Renaissance and now turn to the differing approach of Dr. Rowand Anderson. There must be no comparison between the importance of these two architects —only their approach. It must be remembered that David Rhind was at his best in his interpretation of the purely classical. Dr. Anderson is more freely creative in the modelling of his building and thus shows a differing approach to classical motive in his composition. Yet this is no less sincerely derivative from the Italian Renaissance and thus must seek their definition in this period.

Dr. Anderson's career is all the more remarkable in that family pressure when he was a young man brought him to practice Law, much against his own inclination. After some years of this uncongenial employment he became a pupil in the School of the Board of Manufacturers, forerunner of the present Schools of Architecture and Design in Scotland. Employment in various architectural offices followed after which he, in common with many other young architects of his day, studied on the continent where he gained his Mastery of Renaissance Design.

THE McEWAN HALL

The Renaissance of the nineteenth century—The McEwan Hall.

The Royal Observatory

The history of Playfair's building on the Calton Hill is too well documented to warrant its inclusion here, and is in any event out of our period. In contrast, the history of the Royal Observatory on Blackford Hill is obscure and I am by no means satisfied that such research as has been possible is adequate and complete.

A stimulus to astronomical research was given to Edinburgh in 1888 by a gift of instruments and a valuable private library, then in the possession of the Earl of Crawford. The inadequacy of the Calton Hill building was realized and plans prepared for the new building on Blackford Hill. The whole thing is of exceptional interest. Its detailing is irreproachable and as an architectural composition it is highly significant. It does justice to its commanding position and must be recognized as a major contribution to nineteenth-century Edinburgh. The necessity for a precise distance between the two towers, the provision for adequate working space for telescopes and a need for their precise field of operation, with many other details of scientific requirements affecting the design of the building, are an indication of architect Walter W. Robertson's ability to relate function to design.

W. W. Robertson (1846–1907) is an obscure figure despite the importance of many of his works. He was apprenticed to the City Architect of Edinburgh and later went to the firm of Holdern & Sons in Manchester. In 1871 he was appointed technical assistant to Sir Douglas Goulton, the last architect to hold the title of H.M. Director of Works. Robertson later became Chief Architect to H.M. Office of Works in Scotland, which appointment he held until his retirement in 1904. His major buildings include Glasgow General Post Office and Inland Revenue Office, and the creation or extension of official buildings throughout Scotland.

The strict scientific requirements governing the design of the Royal Observatory have in no way inhibited his production of an outstanding example of the Italianate Revival. The substitution of drums for cupolas is fortunate indeed. There are many unanswered questions both on the building and the architect. The stone employed in the construction is unusual to Edinburgh and is reputed to have come from the north of England, though I have no direct evidence of this. Its use is predominant in the general colour and effect of the building and with the sure touch of refined 'Italianate' must reflect architectural sensitivity of a high order. It is possible that the main gate is a later addition.

THE ROYAL OBSERVATION.

The Royal Observatory on Blackford Hill.

3: *Victorian Baroque*

The British Linen Bank

O N the east side of St. Andrew Square, the Royal Bank of Scotland is set back in its own forecourt, flanked by the two small mansion houses faced with Ionic pilasters. The one to the south is number 37 St. Andrew Square, town house of the Countess of Dalhousie until her death in 1807 when the property was acquired by the British Linen Bank. The bank then vacated their Tweeddale Court premises in the Old Town and occupied the Dalhousie mansion in 1808.

The Directors bound themselves '*to keep and preserve the front wall and gable end in the same state and of the same height*'. In those days town planning had some value! This house and its counterpart in the north are attributed to Robert Adam and it is interesting to note again the name of Robert Reid, so often associated with alterations or additions to Adam's work, in connection with internal reconstruction of the bank premises. Needed expansion resulted in the acquistion of number 38, and later of numbers 39 and 40 St. Andrew Square. In 1846 it was decided by the Directors that conditions in the telling-room were intolerable and that rebuilding was essential. Instructions were given to the bank's architect for a new building to be erected to the south of the Dalhousie mansion, connecting and having regard to the Adam building. Again, we can see a concern for architectural good manners. William Burn and David Bryce were commissioned jointly to prepare designs for the new building, though it is generally considered to be the work of David Bryce, as Burn removed his practice to London in 1844.

The building is of considerable interest when closely examined. While the detail is classic in form, it is exuberant and scarcely to be contained within the discipline of the Italianate Revival. The value of the façade lies in the modelling, which is magnificently three-dimensional and whilst the purist may be critical of the proportions of the window openings, they seem proper in their relation to the whole, and the mid-nineteenth-century emphasis in horizontal astragals is correct in punctuation. Here then we have a building of undoubted merit which does not fall easily into the accepted definitions of the period. An examination of the interior and especially of the splendid staircase in the entrance hall suggests that the description *Victorian Baroque* is correct.

THE BRITISH LINEN BANK

The British Linen Bank, St. Andrew Square.

A Contrast in Styles

The familiar silhouette of the Mound and massive Victorian Baroque of the nineteenth-century reconstruction of the Bank of Scotland are possibly among the most well-known aspects of the Edinburgh skyline. The composition of the whole, observed from the head of St. Giles Street, must be less frequently seen and yet is infinitely worth while. The rich classical moulding of the bank is a contrast to the grouping of the Gothic towers of William Playfair's New College and to the left of this is one of the late nineteenth-century tenements, architecture reminiscent of Henbest Capper and the Geddes reconstructions (though I have no information on this). In the distance a grouping of the towers and spires of St. Mary's Cathedral, St. George's West and St. Cuthbert's Parish Church forms the skyline.

The Bank of Scotland, chartered in 1695, was originally in Old Bank Close, which, together with its adjacent buildings, was removed when Bank Street became a thoroughfare linking the Lawnmarket with Princes Street. The first building on the new site was erected in 1806, the architect being Richard Crichton. Its present form is largely the work of David Bryce who was responsible for the alteration and enlargement of the bank in 1870. The composition in every way indicates the refinement associated with David Bryce's work, though one feels that in this instance the architect has been tempted by the grandeur of his site to an opulence wholly fitted to the importance of the building. A richness of modelling suggests Victorian Baroque rather than Italianate, and is justified today when the building is floodlit. Northern skies do not give full significance to Italian exuberance in architectural detail and the thoughtful scheme of floodlighting employed by the bank not only gives value to its architecture but also lends a great deal of colour to it.

Patrick Geddes' sensitive improvements in the Lawnmarket area deserve the gratitude of posterity. It is not possible to be certain which reconstructions were under his precise control but his influence is unmistakable wherever nineteenth-century rehabilitation is seen in this area.

Playfair's Gothic towers of the New College are vital to the Edinburgh skyline; they are also of considerable interest in their association with the Presbyterian Disruption of 1843 (see page 22) and are unique in this architect's work. Thus in a single, and possibly unusual view, we have three singular aspects of Victorian Edinburgh. We should not consider them individually but rather as a group whose harmony is all the more remarkable for the diversity of their conception.

ST GILES ST

The Bank of Scotland from St. Giles Street.

St. George's West

St. George's West in Shandwick Place, Edinburgh, was built to replace a church removed from a site on the Lothian Road, subsequently occupied by the Caledonian Railway Station. The new building was completed in 1869 at a cost of £31,000, a remarkable sum in those days, the more especially when one considers the force and drive of the Free Church movement in that it was able to commence building in such a style only about two decades after the Disruption, on which the Free Church was founded. Here again the architect was David Bryce. As may be expected, his design is bold and original, his touch sure, his decoration opulent and rich. The church interior, Victorian Baroque, is by the same artist responsible for the British Linen Bank.

The exterior is free in its interpretation of the Italianate Style. The Campanile was added in 1822 and owes its originality to the curious dwarf spire. This appendage is so much a part of the familiar west-end scene that it is rarely given critical appreciation. It is suitable enough as the termination to the tower, though a little puzzling in its intention. It would have been more in character with Bryce's work to have achieved something rich in modelling and wholly Italianate in style. It would seem probable that David Bryce's death in 1876 may have been the cause of a departure from his original intention.

Should any criticism be levelled at the expedient of adopting the term Victorian Baroque for the more richly decorated Italianate buildings, consideration may be given to the contemporary description of St. George's West, which compared the church to the work of the great Renaissance architect Palladio. It is comparative description of this nature that has misled the twentieth-century observer, for it introduces a note of absurdity and prevents a critical study of Victorian architecture in its own right.

ST GEORGES WEST

Brian Crossland

St. George's West.

The King's Theatre

The art of the theatre is transitory, a fleeting make-believe, a relaxation from the permanent and inescapable. The beginnings of Christian Drama are associated with the early church and when the players were excluded from sacred precincts, secular mummery found its place in the fairground and market place.

Much has been written about the theatre but little about theatrical buildings or their architects. The open stage of the Elizabethans has only recently been rediscovered in its dramatic possibilities and for the Victorian stage we must turn to the convention established by the Restoration dramatists with the proscenium arch and enclosed theatre with its galleries and boxes. The Victorian theatre, like the Victorian public house, has a design wholly suited to its purpose: an atmosphere of gaiety and richness equally unsuited to mundane affairs, but which is right and proper to the occasion of entertainment. Nothing could be more fitting to this calculated exaggeration than Victorian Baroque.

The King's Theatre is strictly speaking later than our period, being built in the early twentieth century but the rich moulding of the interior decoration, the opulent use of marble and gilding and the contrivance of grandeur are wholly Victorian in the understanding of theatrical atmosphere.

There is something a little sad and incongruous about the empty theatre with its subdued lighting and air of desolation. Thus my drawing was completed during a performance of the Five-Past-Eight Show, all the difficulties of draftsmanship being compensated for by the atmosphere of music, light and illusion, which is the proper occasion for the appreciation of theatre design and decoration.

The King's Theatre.

The Royal Lyceum Theatre

The Royal Lyceum Theatre, built in 1883, contrasts greatly with the King's Theatre. The exterior is finer, the interior comparatively delicate and restrained in its decoration; an interesting contrast each most suitable in its own way. Our reaction to theatre is not influenced by a critical appraisal of design unless this is of special interest. We are in the heightened atmosphere of anticipation, but, make no mistake, unless the surroundings obey the convention of unreality, anticipation is dulled to apprehension and the players have a hard task indeed.

It is arguable that this atmosphere may be achieved in the fantastic pattern of lighting appliances in the web of roof timbering of the General Assembly Hall above its Festival open stage, but the familiar convention of the Victorian stage is heir to three hundred years of unbroken tradition and suitable to an infinite variety of presentation.

The Royal Lyceum Theatre is one for which I have a special affection, not only for its architectural qualities but also for the pleasures of the auditorium. Indeed, I have appeared on its stage, and therefore can speak with experience. That the dressing-rooms are poorly appointed is accepted. The theatre-goer may find himself placed behind one of the columns supporting the gallery, should he accept one of the limited number of seats having this disadvantage. These deficiencies are not irremediable and are no argument for the threatened destruction of this theatre. A stay of execution has been made by the adoption of this theatre by the Municipality. I trust that this will lead to its retention in the Festival City, so inadequately equipped for Festival entertainment, let alone accommodation of such distinction. The very real qualities of the Royal Lyceum are Victorian theatre design and should in themselves demand the accommodation of the new Festival theatre on some other convenient site.

THE ROYAL LYCEUM THEATRE

The Royal Lyceum Theatre.

The Victorian Public House

Victorian commercial design at its very best may be seen in the comfortable opulence achieved in the more respectable public house. Of the few remaining in Edinburgh, the Abbotsford in Rose Street is the outstanding example. Victorian Baroque has created and maintained an atmosphere where a luncheon in the national tradition may be anticipated without disappointment and the contents of the cellar ordered with confidence. I do not consider it fanciful to attribute these qualities to the maintenance of character. Where we have seen so many splendid interiors destroyed (at the importunity of the shop fitter) the entertainment has become vapid and the atmosphere uneasy. Not ten minutes' walk from the Abbotsford, a once famous chop-house has been gutted and transformed into a combination of pseudo-continental restaurant with overtones of the ice-cream parlour, a disastrous affair in a city with so few good eating houses and so many diners.

The Victorians were very sure of the tradition that they created in transforming the hospitable inn kitchen or common-room into the traditional public house. The beautifully carved bar furniture and wall panels are irreplaceable in cost today, as also are the heavily coffered ceilings and ornate plaster work. All this gives an air of genuine comfort and richness. The careful contrivance of screens and in certain cases intricately cut glass partitions, heightens the sense of seclusion and comfortable enclosure—a commercial asset so easily seen by a comparison between the traditional and the windy open spaces of the modern establishment with its distasteful chromium and imitation red leatherette.

An outstanding example of the re-creation of Victorian design and atmosphere is the Champion Public House in London. How much more economical it would be to recognize the sure touch of the Victorian designer in his appreciation of good taste and commercial necessity, and to preserve those examples remaining to us. Re-creation of an atmosphere is never wholly satisfactory even if done with consummate skill. Let us give recognition not only to the common sense of the nineteenth-century designer, but also to the irreplaceable qualities of his material and the humanity and comfort of his contrivance.

The Abbotsford, Rose Street.

4: *Victorian Town Planning*

An Opportunity Lost

ST. STEPHEN'S CHURCH, built in 1828 by William Henry Playfair, is ten years out of our period, but its dominating influence as a focal point in the New Town of Edinburgh leads us to consider the lost opportunity, which later New-Town planning should have grasped, in extending nineteenth-century development to the north and east of the New Town. Playfair's extraordinarily clever solution for his difficult site clearly envisaged the island position of his church as a focal point for an extension of the New Town.

The drawing is taken from Fettes Row, bounded on the south side by decayed but admirable Georgian buildings, and having its axis visually on St. Stephen's Church. It was the obvious intention for future development to continue a residential street in this direction. Minor commercial developments occupy the northern side of the street and the vista is partially blocked by a furniture store and some inconsequential housing. Here indeed is a lost opportunity in planning. It was clearly intended that Fettes Row should be continued so as to leave St. Stephen's free standing with further early nineteenth-century domestic development grouped round the church to the north.

The advantage of this arrangement would not only have been visually splendid but, in a later age, practical from the point of view of traffic circulation. Perhaps it is not too late to consider the removal of the commercial and domestic buildings which have intervened. Not only would a free standing St. Stephen's be visually enhanced, but a possible inner traffic route would be opened up without the damage to the New Town usually associated with such schemes.

Such an ideal solution would assume that the architectural treatment would be mannerly in conforming to the scale and proportion of the New Town. This idea is by no means impossible but its realization would necessitate a consideration of the proprieties, which is improbable in current architectural taste. This could best be achieved by placing the scheme in the hands of an architect-planner of international reputation.

FETTES ROW

Fettes Row.

The New Town Extension

While it has been generally accepted that James Craig's eighteenth-century plan for the New Town of Edinburgh had set an inimitable standard in civic art, the later nineteenth-century additions to the west of Craig's plan are less praised, when in fact they should receive comparable recognition as an exercise in town planning. Craig's plan stimulated the architects of his period, the culminating feature of their achievement being Robert Adam's Charlotte Square, which has rightly been described as the finest example of continuous domestic architecture in Europe. This may be said without detriment to the remaining architectural compositions, covering the largest area of faultless Georgian design in the British Isles. What must be generally regarded as the New Town extension is largely the development of the Walker estate of Drumsheugh, west of the Queensferry Road. This development commenced around 1820 and continued until about 1880. As with the original New Town, the plan was laid out and the architectural composition controlled by well-informed architectural direction.

The sure grasp of eighteenth-century delicacy of detail is not evident in later nineteenth-century taste. The Italianate style has supplanted the secure grasp of form and detail. Yet fundamental principles in architecture and planning are observed and it is necessary to give this New Town the respect which is its due. The general principles of architectural composition, the proportion of window openings to wall space, the punctuation and termination of streets, the siting of principal buildings and so forth is irreproachable. I will refer to a quotation for the late Professor Sir Patrick Abercrombie, one of the most distinguished planners of this century. Referring to civic design in the United Kingdom he says: *The most extensive example of domestic space planning is the New Town of Edinburgh; built in several stages (the first by Craig), it makes London and continental residential planning look bald and jejune in comparison with its interest, its varied arrangements and shapes. In none of these examples from London, Bath or Edinburgh was through traffic considered; indeed it would be the aim of the designer to exclude it, or at any rate not to encourage it.*

It is infinitely sad that a proper recognition of these fundamentals is seldom held by planning authorities. The entire area of the New Town, both eighteenth century and nineteenth, is unique in its architecture and planning, and cannot be regarded as the property of Edinburgh or even Scotland, but is rather of international importance.

The New Town Extension—Chester Street.

Boldness and Drama

The opening of Bank Street, cutting through the High Street to make a connection with the Mound, was completed in 1798. This swept away Old Bank Close, original site of the Head Office of the Bank of Scotland, and so gave us the splendid building occupying a commanding site at the head of the Mound. The original was designed by Richard Crichton and completed in 1806, but to all intents and purposes the reconstruction of the building in 1868 to 1870 gives us yet another building by David Bryce. The refinement of classical detail is typical of this architect, but in this instance the richness of modelling and opulence of design suggests the description *Victorian Baroque*.

George IV Bridge, like the South Bridge, is literally a street on a bridge and is carried on a series of arches spanning the valley between the Castle Ridge, on which the old town of Edinburgh stands, and the opposing rise on which the University Old Quad is centred. This imaginative exercise in town planning gives us dramatic views from the Cowgate. The opportunity given to today's planners by this splendid conception presents an opening which should not be disregarded.

The ancient buildings of the Cowgate have been demolished in slum clearance and the possibilities of the site suggest a progressive reconstruction fitting to the capital city of Scotland. It would be appalling if the considerable powers of planning control were not applied to give as careful consideration to this area as they have exercised in the Royal Mile and the New Town. The opportunity for re-creation has been ably grasped in the Royal Mile. Could not a similar exercise of a revival of Scottish Vernacular be attempted in this area, combined with rehabilitation of the ancient buildings of the West Bow and Grassmarket?

The drawing gives some indication of the authority of an earlier generation of planners. It is significant that a glimpse is obtained of Washington Browne's Central Library. This notable building is in itself a warrant for sufficient care in determining redevelopment.

The Cowgate, east of George IV Bridge.

An Opportunity Grasped

Victoria Street was part of the same planning scheme which opened up Bank Street, and in which the George IV Bridge spanned the valley of the Cowgate. It connects with the ancient West Bow, the few remaining buildings of which may be seen at the lower end of the street, and whose preservation is well worthwhile. Victoria Street, at its junction with George IV Bridge, is a model of town-planning principle. The raised walk and colonnade is a safe and satisfactory solution to the problems of the site which should be noted by our modern planners. The building which turns the angle of the street and fronts on to the bridge is part of a scheme which is skilfully devised to connect with, and retain, the ancient buildings of the Lawnmarket. Restoration of these in recent years has emphasized the skill of the Victorian planners in effecting their improvements with due regard to the character of the city.

On the left of the street is India House. This has recently been restored and is an enlightened example of Victorian preservation. The building was erected some hundred years ago to the design of David Cousin, then City Superintendent. At this time the City Superintendent was permitted to undertake private commissions, a relaxation of official restriction which must have broadened creative ability, and is, alas, no longer practicable today, however desirable in principle. From the early 1920's the building was occupied by the Loyal Order of Ancient Shepherds, and therefore adequately maintained. This is one Victorian house whose merit has been seen and whose restoration was carried out with sensitivity and a realization of its value. For this we must thank Mr. John G. Gray.

Regrettably such perception is all too rare today. Many, and even more architecturally valuable buildings, could be maintained in useful occupation to the visual benefit of the city and the commendation of future architectural historians. It is a matter of infinite regret that the building fronting George IV Bridge between Victoria Street and the Lawnmarket has not been recognized for its qualities, and thus rehabilitated. Until our authorities are aware that decay in no way affects architectural design, and an appreciation of true values precedes thoughtless demolition, we must continue to witness the destruction of a heritage too recent to have received full recognition.

VICTORIA STREET

Visual effect of town planning conducted with unrestricted competence—Victoria Street.

Leith Street

The view illustrated by this drawing is an example of the possibilities of site planning dictated by difficult topography. Our forebears were not deterred by steep slopes, and found a ready answer to the problems of under-building. The result is interesting both architecturally, and also in the natural movement of the individual who always views architecture in movement and thus sets plane against plane, which is the essence of architectural appreciation.

The tower of the North British Hotel is the dominant feature of this view. The massing of the building is adequate to the site while the tower is wholly acceptable in its relationship both to Princes Street and the head of Leith Walk. The detailing of the building is a remarkable complex of late Victorian design, wholly of its period, owing something to the classical, something to the architecture of confidence, and in the variety of its roofline there is a hint of the Second Empire.

The supremely confident solution for the turning of the corner at the junction of Leith Street is a measure of nineteenth-century competence. An octagonal tower terminates the terrace and there is a raised pedestrian walk to the houses. In the foreground we see a wedge-shaped architectural terminal where the vista sweeps away on either side on different levels, the left leading to the Waterloo Bridge and architecture of an earlier period. Here is the Black Bull Tavern from which the coaches left for England in the days when the main road south had its first posting house at the Howgate Inn.

With the exception of Adam's Register House and Waterloo Place, none of this is individually distinguished architecture. The composition and character of this basically nineteenth-century scene has an attraction which will be recognized and admitted. Its destruction is a matter of time, and its replacement cannot be anticipated with confidence. Even if it were possible to visualize architecture of comparable scale and effect, the regulations governing building today would hardly permit so satisfactory a solution, visually or practicably.

An exercise in varying planes—Leith Street.

Princes Street

The building of Princes Street was started in the last years of the eighteenth century. Craig's New Town planned George Street as the main shopping street, and Princes Street as purely residential. A height clause was embodied in the legislation, and it was not until the mid-nineteenth century that this was rescinded, and buildings of commercial and public importance began to break the regular terraces of domestic housing.

The remains of the original Princes Street may be clearly seen in many of the houses where upper stories are above modern shop fronts. The frontage of the one-time News Cinema is embellished with pilasters, added by a retired Admiral who considered this distinction necessary to his establishment. Some few years ago I discovered box beds in the upper storey of a house between Castle Street and Frederick Street, and there is a finely moulded ceiling remaining miraculously within the shell of a wholly reconstructed modern department store. Most romantic of all is a doorway with an elegant pediment, the whole well preserved and inviting to enter, but which leads nowhere and is never opened!

This is deservedly one of the most famous streets in the world. Some of its most notable buildings are Victorian, others only removed from this period by a few short years. St. John's Church, built in 1816, is a restrained Perpendicular Gothic, original in its construction and charming in its effect; altogether preceding the Gothic Revival proper. The R.S.A. Galleries at the foot of the Mound were completed in their present form in the accession year of Queen Victoria. The Italianate architecture of the major clubs is distinguished.

The two great department stores of Jenner's and R. H. Forsyth are examples of nineteenth-century exuberance. Jenner's was built in 1895, following the fire which destroyed their premises in 1892, and was designed by W. Hamilton Beattie. Mr. Beattie claimed that his design had its origins in the Bodleian Library in Oxford. This extravagance hardly does justice to his creation, which is wholly late Victorian Baroque and is a transitional design marking the turn of the century and the creation of the architecture of confidence.

PRINCES STREET EDINBURGH.

Princes Street.

59

A Guide to Development

One of the more distinguished architects of the early nineteenth century created certain prominent buildings in the London Road area pointing to a clearly defined plan for future development which has not been fully realized. Early nineteenth-century additions have not proved unworthy but should suggest a nucleus in areas where redevelopment is necessary, and provide a stimulating exercise for modern planners in realizing the possibilities of the original scheme. This, of course, should include rehabilitation of nineteenth-century properties suited to this exercise and enable all Playfair's foresight in his architectural compositions to be recognized.

This is an isolated example of New Town development at the junction of London Road with Leith Walk. Its possibilities are tremendous. Playfair's architectural prominence is unquestioned, and his solution for the western termination of London Road and its northern continuation into Elm Row must be seen as part of the New Town of Edinburgh.

A height restriction was imposed on the single-storey houses at the left of the drawing. I am uncertain as to whether this was advisable as a proper continuation of the corner block might well have been effective. However, the scale and appearance of this terrace is acceptable, and whilst clearly not a part of Playfair's plan, is an accident which may well be regarded as satisfactory.

Elm Row (the continuation of the east side of Leith Walk north of London Road) is part of Playfair's design and the buildings opposite on the west side of Leith Walk are acceptable. It is in the eventual redevelopment or rehabilitation of the south side of the Walk to the junction of Broughton Street that care should be taken to respect the work of one of the greatest architects of the New Town.

This whole area was obviously intended as an extension to the eighteenth-century New Town. If this promise was not fulfilled it was probably due to social rather than planning reasons and recognition of Playfair's valuable architecture is a pointer to the line on which rehabilitation and development should take place.

London Road.

5: *The Adventurous and Unusual*

The Tudor Revival

JAMES DONALDSON of Broughton Hall, who died on 9th October 1830, willed the whole of his property to found a hospital for the care of orphaned and destitute children and a Trust was formed to administer the project. The Trustees asked three architects to prepare plans—James Gillespie Graham, David Hamilton of Glasgow and William Henry Playfair. Seventeen acres of ground were purchased in the Coates Estate, and Playfair was commissioned to carry out the project.

William Henry Playfair (1789–1857) made a major contribution to nineteenth-century Edinburgh. His completion of Robert Adam's Old Quad for Edinburgh University; outstanding street architecture in Regent Terrace, Royal Terrace and Carlton Terrace; his splendid but incomplete plan of the junction of London Road and Leith Street, would alone establish his importance among the major architects whose contributions to the New Town of Edinburgh have established a timeless reputation. Donaldson's Hospital was Playfair's last important work. In its execution we see a phase of Victorian Revival architecture which is unusual in major works in Scotland. It is frankly Tudor in conception.

Playfair himself regarded Donaldson's Hospital as one of his greatest creations. His only other venture into this style is a little gatehouse leading to Heriot's Hospital, and comparisons have sometimes been drawn between the Heriot and Donaldson's Hospital. This, in my view, is entirely mistaken, and can only rob the nineteenth-century building of its true values as an original work. The building was visited by Queen Victoria, when nearing its completion in 1850, and a contemporary report records that *Her Majesty walked by the corridor adjoining the Quadrangle and repeatedly remarked upon the magnificence of the edifice itself*. I find this singularly apposite. My first impression on entering the building was to make a mental note of the extraordinary skill with which the architect had arranged his sight lines and vistas commanding the central courtyard.

The building is now used as a school for deaf and dumb children, and it is gratifying that such a necessary function continues the use of what is certainly the most important building of its style and period in Scotland.

DONALDSON'S HOSPITAL

Donaldson's Hospital.

Cast Iron and Building

Dating from 1812 there was a Natural History Museum in Edinburgh attached to the University and occasionally open to the public. By the middle of the century the intense intellectual consciousness, which gave rise to so many themes in art and discoveries in science, found expression in the Great Exhibition of 1851, for the creation of which His Royal Highness the Prince Consort was so largely responsible. The resounding success of the Exhibition gave an impetus to scientific and cultural displays throughout the United Kingdom. In March 1852, a distinguished deputation from Edinburgh met representatives of the Government to express the need for an Industrial Museum of Scotland. It was suggested that this should also be a museum of the history of the world in special relation to Scotland. In 1858 Parliament voted a sum of £10,000 for the erection of the first part of the new buildings to house the rapidly growing collection which already embarrassed the temporary premises in which it was stored. Plans were prepared for the museum building on the south side of Chambers Street, and work on the site commenced in February 1861.

The foundation stone was laid by the Prince Consort, his last public act, and fittingly so in view of His Royal Highness's exceptional interest in projects of this nature. Without in any way diminishing the extraordinary ability of James Paxton, architect of the Crystal Palace, there is no doubt that the Prince Consort assumed a major responsibility in the planning of this Exhibition building which was the forerunner of innumerable structures of a similar type. Captain F. Fowke of the Royal Engineers was unquestionably influenced by Paxton in his preparation of plans of the Royal Scottish Museum. The central Exhibition Hall is possibly the most important example in Edinburgh of the newly discovered use of cast iron. Robert Mathieson, Surveyor to the Board of Works, was the architect for the building and his rather pedestrian Italianate exterior compares less favourably with his New Register House (page 30) and General Post Office. It is possible, however, that his influence in the detailing of the central Exhibition Hall has given us that significance in design which raises it above a purely engineering achievement. For all the seeming fragility of this hall, it is perfectly stable to the eye; and it is of course essential that architecture should give the impression of stability, or it becomes uncomfortable. Modern experiments in design made possible by an advance in constructional methods convey an impression of restlessness to the viewer: a lightening of detail or application of ornament can easily redeem this, and it is exactly on these principles that the composition of the Exhibition Hall rests.

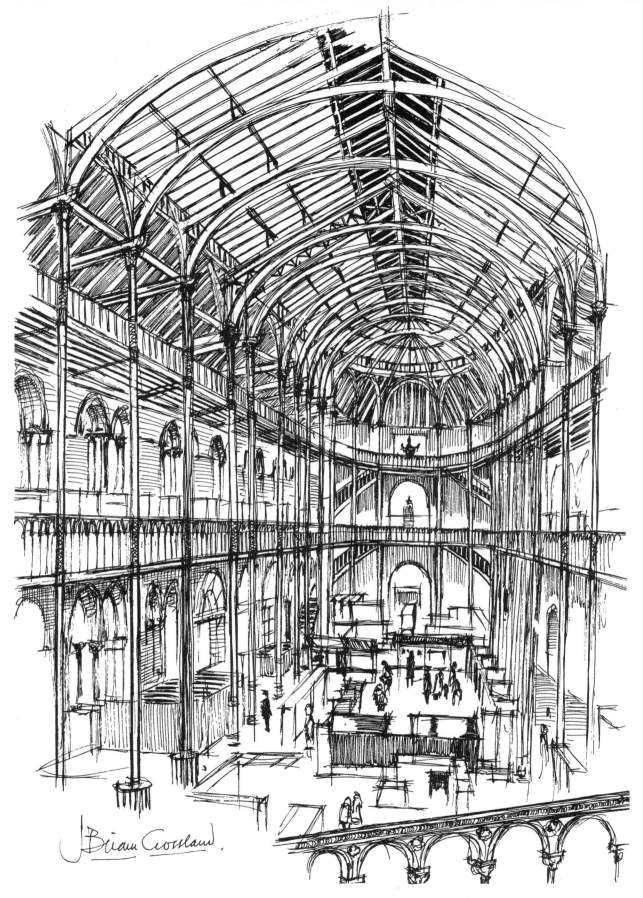

E

The Royal Scottish Museum, Chambers Street.

Diversity of Achievement

This section deals not with a style or a period or a development but with the work of one man, Hippolyte Blanc, whose creations are sufficiently varied to arouse a speculative interest in his personality. Normally, a painter or an architect brings an individuality to his work which is immediately recognizable to those to whom it is familiar. Here we have an architect whose buildings defy easy identification and carry only a subtle degree of continuity in detail.

Hippolyte Blanc restored the great Hall of Edinburgh Castle and added the top storey to the Argyll Tower. This is the slightly incongruous little turret which is the highest point of the Castle and was built in ashlar* deliberately to contrast with the original stonework. Here we see at once an example of the thoughtful consideration for detail which is the thread running through this architect's work. Our respect must grow in examining his extensions to St. Cuthbert's Church at the West End. The original Georgian tower has been retained and it is not certain to what degree Blanc worked on the main body of the original church. His whole nineteenth-century Italianate east end is married to the earlier church with such consummate skill that homogeneity is achieved while considerably enriching the whole.

Mayfield North Church could hardly be more contrasting in style. It has the same authority as the best of the Gothic Revival but is continental in its flavour and displays much originality. Though it could hardly have received the approval of the strict Ecclesiological School it must be regarded today as a building of great originality and importance. On the other hand, Christ Church at Morningside is so contrasting in its Gothic forms that it is hardly recognizable as a work of the same architect. Within a distance of a few hundred yards, the slightly debased Italianate of the red-sandstone church, now recently reconstructed as the People's Theatre, is again in complete contrast. Only in the sensitive detailing of the ornamental panels breaking the wall surface on either side of the front entrance, do we see evidence of the architect's absorption in thoughtful detail.

In this brief account there is evidence of an extraordinary genius. That the work of Hippolyte Blanc has not received wider recognition is due to the unusual qualities to which I have referred. His inclusion in this chapter is fitting as he has all the virtues of the adventurous and curious (see Appendix 4).

* *See page* 92.

MAYFIELD CHURCH

Mayfield North Church.

The Lion and The Unicorn

The monumental columns which stand at the *east* end of Melville Drive were designed by John Lessels and erected in 1881 by Messrs. Thomas Nelson the publishers (a gift to the City in gratitude for the consideration shown to them at the time of the fire which destroyed their Hope Park premises). It was following this fire that the company built the Parkside works which they occupy today). A few years ago the columns were taken down to permit road works to be carried out and it is a matter for some satisfaction that they were subsequently re-erected at a site a little removed from their original position directly at the road junction.

The octagonal columns at the *west* end of Melville Drive were erected to give a formal entrance to the International Exhibition held in the Meadows in 1886. The columns were built by Master Builders and Operative Masons, and stone was used from seventeen quarries in Scotland and the north of England. Each is inscribed with its place of origin and the columns are surmounted by unicorns, the whole being designed by Sir James Gowans.

Returning to John Lessels, his career was most interesting, and yet the details are not usually known. He was born in Kirkcaldy in 1809 and educated at the local school where the schoolmasters were successively Edward Irving and Thomas Carlyle. Carlyle's reputation has survived but the Rev. Edward Irving is less known though celebrated enough in his lifetime (see Appendix 2).

Lessels was trained in the office of William Burn. In 1846 he commenced practice on his own and was later associated with David Cousin as one of the joint architects to the Trust appointed under the Edinburgh Improvement Act. He was therefore responsible for much of the nineteenth-century reconstruction of the land adjoining the High Street. Lessels also produced the feu plan for the lands of Drumsheugh and thus had a hand in the New Town extension. He unsuccessfully submitted designs for St. Mary's Cathedral, though it is believed that his contribution only narrowly missed acceptance. He is also said to have been a painter of some distinction, although I have never seen any of his work. Lessels was certainly a leading figure on the nineteenth-century scene. Yet none of the above information is available in the ordinary sources of reference and it is a measure of the obscurity of nineteenth-century architectural history that this should be so.

Lessels' Columns, Melville Drive.

Scottish Baronial

The adventurous spirit of the Victorian age led its designers into fearless experiment. The architects had a clear understanding of historic precedent and used this in their best compositions, where creative originality is all too often contemporaneously described in terms wildly inaccurate as to architectural style and in disregard of creative composition. This lowered the value of comparative criticism of Victoriana in the first half of the twentieth century and only now is a belated recognition of the finest nineteenth-century examples accorded some significance. And so far this is hardly extended to revivalist Scottish Baronial.

My drawing illustrates a striking example of this style, a mansion house designed by John Lessels. Its silhouette in the evening light is most commanding. Its scale and detail are carried out with confidence and achieve exactly what they were intended to achieve—a Victorian house, designed in the fashion of Scottish Baronial and necessarily giving a standard of comfort and convenience suited to its nineteenth-century occupiers. The mansion house is St. Leonard's, originally built for Thomas Nelson, the publisher, and now a hostel for university students. The proportions of the rooms are admirable and the main staircase is a period piece beyond reproach. This latter may be styled Victorian Baroque, the design bearing no relation to the classical in detail, but only in its conception of splendour. The ceilings will probably delight some future architectural historian if they are preserved. The window openings may be criticized on strictly purist principles but must be accepted as conveniently letting in a great deal of light in conformity to the standard of comfort of the period. The decorated ceiling in the main hall incorporates four medallions with likenesses of the Duke of Argyll, the Earl of Moray, John Knox and the Duke of Montrose. I cannot believe that even Victorian earnestness really considered this a suitable combination. I sympathize with the Duke of Montrose for the thought that he, unlike the others, would probably have appreciated this unconscious pleasantry.

There is a curiously persistent legend that the cap house to the tower was included to remind Mr. Thomas Nelson of the cottage of his birth. Such improbable stories give much harmless pleasure in their relation.

St. Leonards, Dalkeith Road.

Monumental Gothic

Some years ago a distinguished architect of my acquaintance made a profound comment on the Scott Memorial. He said that he could not approve of it architecturally, but nevertheless he would gladly subscribe to any fund for its maintenance should the fabric become decayed.

In the strictest sense of architectural propriety it is of course anomalous that Gothic architectural forms should be divorced from the original needs and intentions of their creators, and contrived, however skilfully, into a massive monumental erection. We should consider the Scott Memorial in terms of its suitability to town-scape and of its function in expressing the reason for its creation, and thus we shall no doubt see why my friend regarded its preservation as so essential.

As a monumental pile, it is a unique and splendid addition to a unique and splendid street justifiably known and affectionately regarded throughout the world. The use of Gothic forms are an adequate tribute to one whose interest in the romantic is reflected in the imaginative contrivance of Gothic Romanticism into a most satisfying composition. Surely this is justification for taking a serious view of the merits of the Memorial? It would be quite wrong in my opinion to deny the adventurous spirit of the Victorian architect who produced such a noticeable feature of the Edinburgh scene, accepting its worthiness while denying its architectural significance. The monument was not admired by John Ruskin, and no doubt he equally disapproved of Mr. George Kemp, referred to in contemporary accounts as a self-taught architect and stonemason. His commission to design a monument which cost £16,000 in 1840 was in itself a remarkable circumstance in a city rich in the architectural talent of the day. The aura of romance and tragedy surrounding the memorial to the Wizard of the North is further enhanced by the untimely death of its creator who was drowned in the Edinburgh-Glasgow Canal before this apex of his achievement was completed.

Various additions were made to the structure until the 1880's, in the form of statuettes and medallions representing characters in the Waverley Novels, and the likenesses of the Scottish poets. The statue of Sir Walter Scott was created by the sculptor Steell and includes the likeness of the poet's dog, Maida. Appropriately, pure romance surrounds the conception and completion of this edifice, although this should in no way prevent us from making a critical appreciation of the Scott Memorial which should lead us to a proper recognition of its qualities.

The Scott Memorial.

Medieval Romanticism

Miss Mary Barclay of 7 Carlton Terrace, Edinburgh, who died in 1858, willed a Trust for the erection of a Free Church of Scotland. The seventeen Trustees were directed to select a suitable site in one of the streets in the New Town of Edinburgh. This provision was later set aside by codicil, and after consideration of sites at Warriston, St. Leonards and the Grange, an agreement was reached with the Fountainbridge Free Church for occupation of the present site in Bruntsfield Place. It was stipulated that the building should be called the Barclay Church.

A competition was held for the design of the church, limited to six chosen architects, and conditions were laid down that the stone was to be used from either Binny or Redhill Quarries, and that the doors were to be sheltered as far as possible from winds. The cost was not to exceed £8,000. The award was made to Frederick Thomas Pilkington in October 1861, together with the first premium of fifty pounds.

The Barclay Kirk owes nothing to the Gothic Revival. Its best description is *Medieval Romanticism*. The body of the church is admirably suited to the Scottish Liturgy. Towering galleries form a half-circle centred on the minister's rostrum and pulpit, the organ being properly placed to the rear of the gallery. This arrangement is both functional and acoustically sound; and the whole centre area of this circular church is free from structural encumbrances. The massive structure of the commanding tower is supported on four main columns situated at the perimeter of the church. Cast-iron pillars in the adjoining rooms play their part in supporting the gallery, but of course are outside the body of the church proper.

Around this functional church interior are massed the soaring pinnacles of Victorian Romanticism culminating in the lofty needle of the tower whose interior is a web of timber exhibiting the engineering ability of the architect. It is regrettable that so many of the exterior mouldings are absent from the stonework. It is popularly believed that this is due to the need for economy, but this is not the case. The minister in charge held a conscientious abhorrence for ornament, and whilst we may admire his determined adherence to principle, it is regrettable that what must appear narrow-mindedness has rendered this church incomplete.

The Barclay Church.

6: *Fin de Siècle*

Washington Browne

It is now necessary to attempt an assessment of the architecture of the final years of the nineteenth century. This is no easy task as one must define a style which is at once wholly individualistic and wholly contemporary. For this complex subject I have selected an appraisal of Sir George Washington Browne, an architect of great prominence whose life span extended from 1853 to 1938. His works include such important commissions as the King Edward VII Memorial at Holyrood Palace, the extension to the Advocates' Library and the Central Library on George IV Bridge.

Washington Browne was born in Glasgow and as a young man was apprenticed to the London architect, John Stevenson. In 1879 he became the principal assistant to Dr. Rowand Anderson, a considerable appointment for a young man of twenty-six. When he opened his own office, he at once fulfilled the promise of his early training and displayed his able grasp of architectural principle in creating outstanding works in the contemporary idiom. Washington Browne's style was not influenced by his predecessors, save in his grasp of architectural history. He was concerned with the architecture of his time; modern, yet securely founded in well-tried tradition. This is not the rediscovery of the Vernacular which found its expression in the comfortable Edwardian house. Nor is it the revolt against mechanization of the Morris School. It is the architecture of the later Victorian Establishment, adventurous in its use of traditional design and motives whilst claiming the convenience of plate-glass and modern architectural planning.

The drawing well illustrates a contrast in Victorian architecture. On the left is the rich modelling and opulent classicism of Victorian Baroque of the Head Office of the British Linen Bank. In the centre, is the Prudential Assurance Building of Sir Alfred Waterhouse, with its equal exuberance of decoration, yet less conscious of its origins, infinitely more restrained in dimension and essentially a creative expression of its period. There is nothing unique about this building and only in individual interpretation does the design differ from the characteristic style of the later Victorian Establishment. The skilful massing of shapes relieved by great freedom of decoration and incrustation of motif is characteristic of a style difficult to define. It is possible to suggest its origins in the inventions of the Second Empire, though it is not directly derivative.

ST ANDREW SQUARE

St. Andrew Square.

77

The Social Conscience

The group of houses and community hall known as Well Court, situated in the Dean Village, is an example of architectural distinction allied to social conscience. Improvement in housing conditions has been established in a close-knit community and the overall concept is wholly in accord with the exceptional surroundings of the Dean Village whilst retaining a desirably urbane character. The model scheme of Well Court was founded by Mr. J. R. Findlay, for many years associated with The Scotsman Publications. Mr. Findlay's house over-looked the village of Dean, much of which he considered to be uninhabitable, requiring complete clearance and rehabilitation. In the early 1880's Mr. Findlay acquired the property occupying the site on which Well Court stands and a scheme for model working-class dwellings was prepared by his architect Mr. Sydney Mitchell. If no other evidence of Victorian competence and sensibility has been given in these pages, this essay in planning technique contrasts in every way favourably with the often fumbling approach of the mid-twentieth century.

Well Court is typical of the architecture of the late nineteenth century. It is essentially Scottish in its general conception, yet unmistakably in accord with its period, where the sense of craftsmanship and scale was in conscious aesthetic revolt against the increasing mechanization of the age. Designers were aware of the receding influence of craftsmanship, the human scale and individualism associated with the craftsman. The influence of William Morris was strongly felt in all fields of art. Voysey established the vernacular in domestic architecture and Sir Ebeneza Howard contributed the Garden City Dream.

The strong bright flame of 'Art Nouveau', the culminating phase of a design movement reaching from William Blake through the pre-Raphaelite period, burned brightly to swift conclusion, but affected almost all forms of creative art of this period. Rennie MacIntosh and the Glasgow School of Architecture and Painting were also strongly influenced by this movement. It is rarely seen in the conservative atmosphere of Edinburgh, but Well Court and Ramsay Gardens both reflect the genius of this phase of the late nineteenth century, and are more than indicative of the extraordinary diversity of creative endeavour from 1837 to 1901.

WELL COURT

Well Court.

The Humanity of the Vernacular

It may not be generally realized that the intricate arrangement of gables, towers and balconies at the western end of Castle Hill, which is so familiar a sky-line from Princes Street, was built as recently as 1892. A closer examination of the architectural arrangement will of course reveal its period as recent, and the style *Romantic* rather than *Traditional*. At the close of the century, a revulsion against increasing industrialization found its expression in the encouragement of hand craftsmanship by leading designers and the potency of 'Art Nouveau'.

I can recall no better example of the humanity of the Vernacular applied to urban architecture than Ramsay Gardens. It was the creation of Patrick Geddes, biologist, sociologist and town planner. The architect was Professor Henbest Capper, though one must assume that the influence of Geddes was strong in the creation of this group of University Halls of Residence and self-contained flats for the University Faculty.

Geddes' interest in social planning in the 1880's did not confine itself to the remedy of civic decay, but embraced his conception of a full university life, where learning allied itself to community living. At that time the student was entirely dependent on private lodgings, often unbelievably poor in quality. The reformer did not merely preach the renaissance of existing academic method, but founded his dream of a co-operative academic life by leasing three tenement flats in the Lawnmarket for the accommodation of students. This modest beginning became in time University Hall, which spread to other buildings in the locality and saw its final achievement in Ramsay Gardens. Here a summer school of art and science was held which achieved an international reputation. It is heartening that part of Ramsay Gardens continues the original academic function as a residential hostel for banking students. Ramsay Gardens has been described as *the most striking monument to Patrick Geddes in the whole city*.

The greatness of Geddes is still recognized today at a period of time when his contribution might well have become outmoded had not his principles been so fundamental to the whole process of social planning. That this process was allied to the human in architectural composition allows us to cherish the hope that it is not too late for the planning of today to return to the correct principles of Geddes and the ideals of the enthusiastic young men of the late nineteenth and early twentieth century.

RAMSEY
GARDENS

Ramsay Gardens.

The Architecture of Confidence

The architecture of Edinburgh, of whatever period, cannot be examined without reference to the magnificent site on which the town is built. Nor must it be forgotten that the splendid massing of Edinburgh's sky-line and its distinctive town planning are not accidental but are due to the skilful solution which the architects and planners of an earlier age applied to the site. How many shoppers strolling along South Bridge are aware that in reality they are crossing a huge viaduct of twenty-two arches spanning the valley between the opposing hills on which the High Street and the University are built and that this was constructed as early as 1788?

The decision to build the New Town of Edinburgh made the construction of a bridge spanning the valley of the Nor' Loch a necessity. The Loch was drained and construction of the bridge started in 1768. The work was delayed for some reason and later in 1769 a considerable portion of the incomplete structure collapsed. It was completed within a few years. Nineteenth-century progress demanded the entire reconstruction of the old bridge and this was done between 1894 and 1897. This is the bridge that we know today, constructed of iron girders and decorated with ornamental cast-iron work. The Victorians so well understood the decorative treatment of their modern materials in producing a sense of scale and lightness. This is especially noticeable in their treatment of cast iron, an uncompromising material at the best of times. A recognition of the ability of the Victorians to give architectural treatment to engineering subjects could provide an object lesson to the engineer-architects of today, and enable them to lighten the desolate weight of their tall structures, which all too often have a restless appearance of instability through lack of acceptable architectural detailing.

The view taken by the drawing is one I particularly admire when considering the buildings flanking the widened North Bridge. The architectural modelling of the *Scotsman* building masses up and up in fascinating shapes to the sky-line. The detail is neo-classic: the composition is that of the architecture of confidence. This, with the Carlton Hotel and Patrick Thomson's store, is architecture suitable to an Empire on which the sun never set. It is the architecture of confidence, built in a secure world to be timeless and to speak with modest grandeur of a settled and well-ordered world. The *Scotsman* building was completed in 1905, just beyond our period, but its whole conception is within the spirit of the climax of the Victorian era.

MARKET STREET

The 'Scotsman' Building.

The Last Phase of the Gothic

Here then is our last look at the Gothic. The Museum of Antiquities, built between 1885 and 1890, is the work of Dr. Rowand Anderson and the building is magnificently nineteenth century. It owes nothing to the ecclesiastical Gothic Revival nor to the romanticism of Pilkington. It is the end and peak of the period. Contemporary opinion speaks of the building as 'fourteenth-century Italian Gothic'. I will not quarrel with this description in so far as it contains the elements of truth, but it is hopelessly wrong in detecting certain elements of design or detail and imprisoning the description of the building within a form of words which allows no freedom to appreciate the composition on its own terms.

An enthusiasm for the High Renaissance which may be traced in certain later nineteenth-century thought, is reflected in the work of some of the pre-Raphaelite painters and equally in the design of some of the jewellery and supposedly Florentine metal ornaments of the period. This is quite different from the widespread Italianate Revival whose affect can be seen throughout the Victorian Period, most markedly in domestic housing. If, then, the sponsors of the Museum of Antiquities were motivated by this higher criticism they could hardly have appointed a more suitable architect, whose appreciation of the artistic supremacy of fifteenth-century Florentine, influences his design concept as surely and sincerely as Pugin or Scott in their great mastery of the Gothic.

It is in this mastery of styles that the contemporary description has once again failed us as a means of assessment. The Museum of Antiquities is a modern building whose elements of design are influenced by an appreciation of historic precedent, as indeed all important architectural composition should be. It is a disregard for historic precedent, and the lack of intellectual devotion to a chosen theme, that makes contemporary architectural design suspect in its intentions, if not downright unarchitectural. The desire to dominate by sheer size, or to shock by restless seeming suspensions of huge masses of concrete, is no substitute for thoughtful detailing nor should a scale adapted to humanity be disregarded. It is on this note that I close with a plea for closer examination of the true values of Victorian buildings. It is only natural that the protagonist of the multi-storey rectangle should pour contempt on the adventurous and varied interests of the nineteenth-century stylist. A passer-by should be no more influenced by this misunderstanding than by the often misleading descriptions applied by the Victorians themselves.

THE MUSEUM OF ANTIQUITIES

The Museum of Antiquities.

Appendix I

Edinburgh and Glasgow—a brief comparison

A full appreciation of Victorian Edinburgh is difficult without a comparative glance at Victorian Glasgow. The extraordinary contrast in emphasis between these two cities gives an essential background to their differing concept of nineteenth-century architecture.

Glasgow has only two major Gothic Revival buildings. I disregard the significance of the splendid church spires as these are rightly conscious of their importance in the town-scape and are allied to buildings of individual modesty. In contrast, Edinburgh is rich in Gothic Revival.

The influence of the Second Empire, which is magnificently displayed in Glasgow and has a world-wide significance, is only modestly seen in Edinburgh in the rooflines of suburban houses and filigree ironwork decorations. Edinburgh at the turn of the century had the architecture of confidence, yet not one single example of 'Art Nouveau'. Glasgow is rich in this rare, subtle and vital movement.

Thus the two cities, only forty-four miles apart, are utterly individual in their nineteenth-century architecture: each in its own way is quite outstanding, but the difference is significant. A realization of this remarkable contrast is necessary if a proper assessment of Victorian values is to be made in either city. Contrast will not be competitive; it will demonstrate the individuality of Victorian architecture and show its values in true perspective.

Appendix 2

Edward Irving

Edward Irving, regarded by his followers as the forerunner of the Catholic Apostolic Church Movement, was born at Annan in Dumfries-shire in 1792. At the age of thirteen he entered the University of Edinburgh and his brilliance as a scholar is attested by the fact that at seventeen he received his Masters' Degree. Later, when he became assistant minister to the renowned Thomas Chalmers in Glasgow, his extrovert preaching won the love and respect of the poor, but elicited little sympathy from Dr. Chalmers. In 1882 he became minister of the Caledonian Church in London's Hatton Garden. In due course, his study of prophecies and mystical obscurantism, derived principally from the Apocalypse, led in 1828 to a series of famous sermons preached in the largest churches of Edinburgh. His impact was as disturbing as that of Newman in Oxford. He was finally excommunicated by the London Presbytery in 1830 and his opinions were condemned by the General Assembly of the Church of Scotland.

In 1832 he became 'Chief Pastor' of a congregation who described themselves as members of the Holy Catholic Apostolic Church. He was then deposed by the Church of Scotland on grounds of heresy and died two years later. The really curious thing is that he did not found 'The Irvingites'. Then and now the members of this Church strongly reject this name.

The liturgical books date from 1842, almost a peak date in the history of Gothic Revivalism. The whole outward ritual of Latin Catholicism was borrowed and the magnificence of its ceremonial drew vast crowds to its great cathedral-like church in Gordon Square, London. This was in the days when Anglican Ritualists were being strongly persecuted. The prevalent idea was that when the last apostle died, the millennium would arrive. When the last apostle did die in 1901, it was held among many that the end of the world would coincide in fact with the death of the last 'angel' or bishop appointed by the 'apostles'.

Appendix 3

Frederick Thomas Pilkington

The Barclay Kirk (page 74) must have been one of Frederick Thomas Pilkington's early works, if not his first, and this architect's work is of extraordinary interest. His originality of conception has aroused antipathy and even levity amongst unresponsive minds. Yet had the Barclay Kirk been his only work of any note, it must eventually have established this man as a genius.

Fortunately we have many other examples of his work both in Scotland and in London, and although his minor works show evidence of less distinguished collaboration, Pilkington's important buildings exhibit an originality of mind allied alike to brilliance of conception and attention to detail.

Frederick Thomas Pilkington was born in 1832 and died in 1899. He was the son of Thomas Pilkington, architect to the Marquis of Exeter, and I understand that the father destroyed his family pedigree, which appeared to him worldly in relation to his Methodist views. The son was articled in London and afterwards attended the University of Edinburgh where he gained the Hamilton prize for Logic and also graduated in mathematics. He spent some time in his father's office in Edinburgh and then commenced practice for himself in 1860.

It is regrettable that so little is known of Frederick Thomas Pilkington the man. Meagre details of his personal life survive and only serve to reinforce the conception of a dedicated personality deeply committed to his profession. He remains an enigma and it rests with us to study the work of his individual genius and respect his claim to historic importance.

IRVINE

The Church at Irvine, Ayrshire, built by Frederick Thomas Pilkington.

Appendix 4

Hippolyte Blanc

Hippolyte Blanc was born in Edinburgh in 1844 of a French father and an Irish mother. He was educated at Heriot's School and apprenticed to the architect David Rhind. In 1865 he was employed by the Office of Works as an Inspector of Ancient Buildings under the care of the Crown. Later he went into private practice on his own account.

As we saw in the third section of Chapter 5, Blanc was capable of immense diversification. Apart from the items already mentioned (see page 66), he was responsible for the Thomas Coates Memorial Church in Paisley, a dominant composition where he exercised his skill in the Scottish Vernacular. A Crown Steeple is included as in the Middle Church in Perth where an even more effective atmosphere of the Scottish Vernacular is achieved. I can recall no other example where what may be termed a Scottish Revivalism has been employed to such effect.

In his house at number 17 Strathearn Place (now the Iona Hotel) Hippolyte Blanc designed a ceiling for his drawing-room of such delicacy that it would be assumed to be late eighteenth-century plaster moulding, were this not impossible in a house of this period.

MARSHALL PLACE PERTH

Brian Cumland

Middle Church, Marshall Place, Perth—an example of a Crown Steeple.

Glossary

Apse A semi-circular or polygonal termination to the chancel of a church.

Ashlar Squared-up masonry regularly coursed and faced smooth.

Astragal A pleasant Scots term for the wooden partitions (glazing bars) separating the panes of a window. In normal eighteenth- or nineteenth-century practice, individual panes were vertical, but in the mid-nineteenth century they were occasionally inserted horizontally, giving a wholly different effect in punctuation.

Axis A term used to indicate the dominant architectural feature from which streets may radiate.

Baroque The term applied to the elaborate architectural styles that developed in different countries in the later Renaissance during the seventeenth century. The term 'Victorian Baroque' indicates the opulent three-dimensional development of the Italianate Revival and is purely a means of expression without direct derivation from the true Baroque.

Classical Orders A distinguishing term given to the three distinctive types of Grecian column, each with its entablature: Doric, Ionic and Corinthian. To this the Romans added the Roman Doric, the Tuscan and the Composite (see opposite).

Coffered Ceiling A ceiling decorated with sunk square or polygonal ornamental panels formed in plaster.

Cupola A domed or polygonal architectural feature crowning a turret.

Pediment The low-pitched gable crowning a classical portico or doorway.

Pilaster A pier supporting a wall surface and decorated in conformity with the architectural style of the building.

Punctuation The ability to define the component parts of an architectural composition and arrest the eye by giving significance and meaning to the whole.

Terminal Feature An important architectural feature which terminates the vista of a street or similar view point.

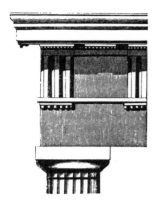

Grecian Doric

Roman Doric

Grecian Ionic

Corinthian

STREET MAP

Key

1. Bristo Street
2. St. James' Church, Leith
3. St. Mary's Cathedral
4. Tolbooth St. John's
5. St. Peter's, Lutton Place
6. The New College
7. National Commercial Bank, George Street
8. Life Association of Scotland Building
9. North British & Mercantile Insurance Building
10. The New Register House
11. The McEwan Hall
12. The Royal Observatory, Blackford Hill
13. The British Linen Bank, St. Andrew Square
14. The Bank of Scotland
15. St. George's West
16. The King's Theatre
17. The Royal Lyceum Theatre
18. The Abbotsford, Rose Street

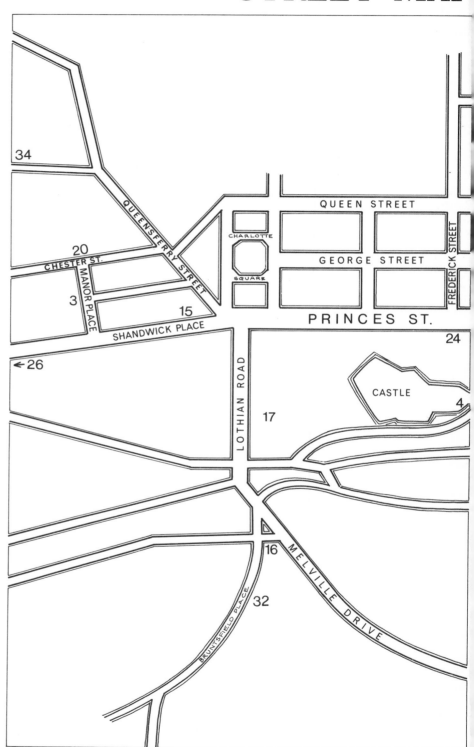

This map has been included to help visitors to

OF EDINBURGH

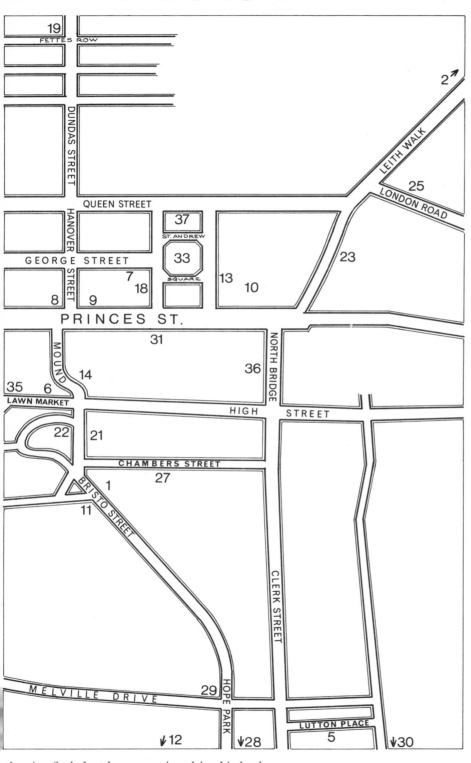

the city find the places mentioned in this book